How to Help Individuals with Autism Flourish

A Comprehensive Guide for Families and Caregivers

Ella C. Martinez

Copyright © Ella C. Martinez, 2024.

Disclaimer

The information provided in this book is for general informational purposes only. While every effort has been made to ensure the accuracy of the information contained within this book, the author and publisher assume no responsibility for errors or omissions, or for damages resulting from the use of the information contained herein.

This book is sold with the understanding that the author and publisher are not engaged in rendering legal, financial, medical, or other professional advice. The reader should consult with a professional in the respective field for any such advice.

Table Of Contents

Introduction

This book is an invaluable resource for parents, caregivers, educators, and anybody looking to gain a better knowledge of autism and learn how to effectively assist and empower people on the spectrum.

As someone who has been through this road, either personally or professionally, you understand that autism is more than simply a diagnosis; it is a distinct way of experiencing the world. Whether you're a parent who has just heard the words "Your child has autism," a teacher working to create an inclusive classroom or a professional working with people on the spectrum, this guide will provide you with the knowledge, tools, and inspiration you need to make a difference.

The Book's Purpose And Scope

The goal of this book is threefold: to provide a full understanding of autism, to offer practical solutions for assisting individuals with autism, and to empower those individuals to thrive. We'll look at the various characteristics and presentations of autism, refute popular beliefs, and discuss the most recent scientific studies on causes and treatments. This book will also bring you through the several stages of support, such as early intervention, educational strategies, vocational training, and self-advocacy. By addressing these many stages, I hope to provide you with a toolset that can be adjusted to each individual's specific needs with autism.

CHAPTER 1

Understanding Autism

What Is Autism?

Autism, often known as autism spectrum disorder (ASD), is a complex, lifelong condition characterized by difficulties with speech and behavior. It is a spectrum condition, which means that it affects people differently and to variable degrees. It normally appears by the age of two or three.

People with autism struggle with communication. They have difficulty comprehending how others think and feel. This makes it difficult for people to express themselves, whether through words, gestures, facial expressions, or touch.

People with autism may struggle with learning. Their skills may develop unevenly. For example, individuals may struggle to communicate but excel at art, music, math, or memory-related tasks. As a result, individuals may excel at analytical or problem-solving assessments.

Autism is being diagnosed in more children now than ever before. However, the most recent figures may be higher due to changes in how the disease is identified, rather than because more children have it.

Autism is classified as "low-functioning" or "high-functioning" Each individual with autism will be influenced differently. Some people struggle with social, learning, and communication skills. They may require assistance with daily duties and, in some situations, are unable to live independently.

Many refer to this as "low-functioning autism." Other people may have autism but exhibit less visible symptoms. They frequently perform well in school and communicate more effectively. People commonly refer to this as "high-functioning autism." However, the words "high-functioning" and "low-functioning" may be derogatory. It is better to avoid them. To discuss how autism impacts someone, you might instead use language like "more significant"

Autism Symptoms

Autism symptoms usually occur before a child turns three. Some people exhibit characteristics from birth.

Common autism symptoms include:
- Lack of eye contact
- A narrow range of interests or a strong interest in specific issues
- Repeating words or phrases, swaying back and forth, or fiddling with items (for example, turning a light switch)
- High sensitivity to noises, sensations, scents, or sights that appear normal to others
- Not looking at or listening to others
- Not looking at items when someone points at you.
- Not wanting to be held or cuddled.
- Difficulties interpreting or using speech, gestures, facial expressions, or tone of voice.
- Speaking in a sing-along, flat, or robotic voice
- Trouble adjusting to routine adjustments Some autistic youngsters may also experience seizures. These might not begin until adolescence.

Autism symptoms in adults

Autism in adults may manifest in distinct ways. Common symptoms may include:

- Having difficulty comprehending what others are thinking or experiencing
- Choosing to remain alone or having trouble forming friends
- Anxiety over social activities
- Difficulty expressing emotions and sticking to a routine
- Taking things literally or misinterpreting sarcasm
- Coming out as blunt, indifferent, or rude to others without intending to

Other indicators of autism in adults may include:

- Avoiding eye contact
- Not comprehending social queues or "rules"
- Getting too close to people or becoming irritated if someone gets too close or touches you
- Having a strong interest in specific things
- Observing subtle nuances, scents, noises, or patterns that others may not notice
- Preferring meticulous planning before action

Autism symptoms in children

Autistic children may present several symptoms. They may include:

- Not responding to their name at the age of 9 months.
- Not displaying facial emotions by 9 months old.
- Not wanting to play basic games (like pat-a-cake) at 12 months of age.
- Does not employ gestures (such as waving hello) by 12 months of age.
- Does not understand when other people are upset or mad by 24 months old.
- Does not notice or wish to join other children to play by 36 months old.
- Does not sing, act, or dance for you by the age of sixty months.
- Lines up toys in a precise order and becomes unhappy when the sequence is disturbed.
- Demonstrates excessive interest
- Rocking their body, flapping their hands, and spinning in circles.
- Delayed language, movement, learning, or cognitive abilities
- Unusual sleeping or eating habits
- Less or more fear of something than would normally be expected.

Stimming

Stimming is a self-stimulating habit that involves hand and arm flapping, rocking, spinning, whirling, jumping, head-banging, and other similar bodily movements. It can also refer to repeatedly using an object, such as flicking a rubber band, spinning a string, caressing anything with a specific texture, and so on.

People with autism may stim for recreational purposes, to relieve boredom, or to cope with stress or worry. It can also help them control the amount of sensory input. For example, kids may twist a thread to observe it or concentrate on one sound to block out another loud or irritating noise.

Meltdowns

A person with autism may become overwhelmed by a circumstance and be unable to respond appropriately. This may trigger them to have a meltdown. They may cry, shout, or physically express themselves by kicking, striking, or biting. They could shut down entirely and stop reacting in any way. This is not a temper tantrum; they are just unable to cope with their feelings or explain them.

Autism Types

These categories were formerly regarded to represent different conditions. Currently, they are classified as autism spectrum disorders, which include:

Asperger syndrome

Children with Asperger's syndrome typically score in the average to above-average range on intelligence tests. However, they may struggle with social skills and have a limited range of interests.

Autistic disorder

This is what most people associate with the term "autism." It has an impact on children's social interactions, communication, and play before the age of three.

Child disintegrative disorder

Children with this disease experience typical growth for at least two years before losing part or all of their speech and social skills. Pervasive developmental condition, often known as atypical autism. Your doctor may use this phrase if your child exhibits some autistic symptoms, such as deficits in social and communication skills, but does not fall into another category.

Autism Causes

Autism's cause is unclear. It could be caused by issues in your brain's sensory input and language processing areas. Autism is four times as prevalent in boys than in girls. It can affect persons of all races, ethnicities, and socioeconomic backgrounds. A child's autism risk is unaffected by his or her family income, lifestyle, or education level.

However, there are some risk factors:

A child with an older parent is more likely to develop autism. Pregnant women who have been exposed to specific substances or chemicals, such as alcohol or anti-seizure medications, are more likely to have autistic children.

Other risk factors include maternal metabolic disorders like diabetes and obesity. Autism has also been related to untreated phenylketonuria (PKU), a metabolic condition caused by an enzyme deficiency, and rubella (German measles).

Is autism a genetic condition?

Autism runs in families, thus certain gene combinations may raise a child's risk. Changes in over 1,000 genes may be connected to autism. However, not all of these have been confirmed by professionals. Genetic factors can influence someone's likelihood of autism by 40 to

80%. Your overall risk is determined by the mix of your genes, environment, your parents' age, and any birth difficulties.

An uncommon gene mutation or chromosomal problem is believed to be the only cause of autism in 2% to 4% of cases. This usually occurs in disorders that affect other sections of the body, such as mutations in the ADNP gene. ADNP syndrome causes a person to have autism symptoms as well as unique facial traits. Many of the genes involved with autism are linked to brain development. This may explain why autism symptoms include difficulties with speech, cognitive functioning, and sociability.

Vaccines and Autism

Vaccines do not cause autism. Despite some people's concerns, research has proved that there is no link between the two. Experts evaluated the safety of eight vaccines for children and adults. They discovered that they were extremely safe, with only a few outliers. Other research examined the components of various vaccines and found no link to autism. Vaccines have considerably greater health advantages than potential hazards.

Autism Tests

Autism can be difficult to diagnose definitively. Your doctor will concentrate on behavior and development. Diagnostic procedures for children often involve two steps. A developmental screening will inform your doctor whether your child is on track for basic skills such as learning, speaking, behavior, and movement.

Experts recommend that children be checked for developmental delays at 9 months, 18 months, 24, or 30 months of age. Children are frequently screened for autism at their 18-month and 24-month exams. If your child shows indicators of a problem during these exams, they will require a more comprehensive evaluation. This may involve hearing and vision exams, as well as genetic studies. Your doctor may recommend that you consult with an autistic specialist, such as a developmental pediatrician or child psychologist.

Some psychologists can administer a test known as the Autism Diagnostic Observation Schedule (ADOS). If you were not diagnosed with autism as a child but are experiencing symptoms, speak with your doctor. If you just received a diagnosis

If you've recently been diagnosed with autism, there are a few things you can do to feel better:

Take the time you need to grasp the diagnosis. You might experience a range of feelings. Know that you can ask your doctor for help. You can live a normal life even after being diagnosed.

Conduct your research. Listen to individuals with autism. There are several resources, books, and videos to help you understand the disease. People with autism can also share their stories, allowing you to learn more about the illness. Get the help you need. If you or your kid feels isolated after obtaining an autism diagnosis, seek help.

National advocacy organizations, support groups, your doctor, autistic individuals on social media, and your school, workplace, or college can all help you navigate a diagnosis. Keep an eye out for additional health issues.

While autism is not an illness, many people with it may also have ADHD, dyslexia, or other conditions. If you have any concerns about your or your child's health, talk to your doctor. Living with autism. Autism is a lifelong condition. However, early intervention can have a substantial impact on a child's development with autism. If you suspect your child has ASD, contact your doctor right away. Autism therapies. Something that works for one individual may not work for another. Your doctor should adapt treatment to you or your child.

The primary type of therapy is Behavioral: Assists a person in understanding the origins and consequences of actions, allowing them to change unpleasant behaviors.

Speech therapy improves communication skills, physical therapy improves motor abilities, and occupational therapy focuses on living skills such as dressing and eating.

Psychological treatments, such as cognitive-behavioral therapy (CBT), can help people deal with anxiety, sadness, or other mental health difficulties. In addition to Autism.

Educational: Customizes learning processes to meet the requirements of individuals with autism.

Social-relational: Concentrates on improving social skills and developing emotional ties.

Medications help to alleviate ASD symptoms such as focus issues, hyperactivity, and anxiety. Complementary therapy may help some autistic people improve their learning and communication skills.

Complementary therapies include music, art, and animal-assisted therapy, such as horseback riding.

Applied behavior analysis (ABA) is a treatment that seeks to encourage desirable conduct while discouraging negative or harmful behavior.

Some experts think that ABA is a sort of behavior control. They claim that it drives people to adhere to a fixed concept of "normal" and suppresses behavior associated with autism. Advocates claim that ABA originated from this technique. They argue that it is the most effective technique for a person with autism to adapt and live more comfortably in society.

Fake Autism Treatments

Certain remedies sold or advertised to treat autism do not work. Some of these bogus treatments can even be harmful. Do not try any of the following for autism:
Raw camel's milk.

GcMAF, an unauthorized injectable derived from blood cells CEASE, advises individuals to forgo immunizations and suggests people take potentially harmful nutritional supplements.

Chlorine dioxide (CD), or Mineral Miracle Solution (MMS) Certain vitamins, minerals, and supplements

Secretin is a hormone in the body, and chelation removes heavy metal poisons from the bloodstream. To identify a bogus therapy, look for these warning signs: Claims of a "cure," "miracle," or "recovery from" autism. It is not available from big, trustworthy health websites. It's very expensive. It claims to help many individuals "instantly." Instead of medical evidence, use personal anecdotes to demonstrate how it worked. Declares that anyone can perform anything, regardless of medical training. It purports to cure a variety of diseases.

Autism disparities

Autism affects distinct categories of people. Autism among women Autism can present differently in women than in males. Compared to men, autistic cisgender women may Hide their feelings. Be quieter. Copy people who don't have autism or disguise their autism symptoms to "fit in" Seems to cope better in social circumstances. Show less evidence of repeated behavior. Your doctor may not be as knowledgeable in diagnosing girls and women with autism.

Many signs of autism are based on masculine stereotypes, making it difficult to determine whether a girl has autism. As a result, girls and women with autism may be misdiagnosed or overlooked outright. As professionals become more aware of this, estimates of the number of males with autism compared to women have decreased. Autism, Racial, and Ethnic Differences White children are more likely to be diagnosed with autism spectrum disorder than Black or Hispanic youngsters. These groups may not receive diagnosis or care for a variety of reasons, including Stigma around the disorder and Reduced access to medical resources due to non-citizenship or income. Not speaking English as their primary language.

LGBTQIA+ and Autism According to research, people with autism are more likely than non-autistic people to identify as LGBTQIA+. People in this group who also have autism are more likely to suffer discrimination, difficulties accessing medical care, violence, and cultural stigma. This may increase the risk of mental health difficulties for LGBTQIA+ people who are autistic. Be cautious about changing your child's diet. Consult your doctor before doing something new, such as a specific diet.

There is no hard evidence that specific diets benefit children with ASD. Autism is a complicated neurological condition. Some children with autism may appear to be fussy eaters. They may only eat foods of a specific color or texture, eat insufficiently or excessively, or consume items that are not food. They may suffer from constipation, which causes them to feel full when they are not, or they may experience coughing or choking while eating. While it may appear that eliminating particular foods can alleviate your child's symptoms, it may actually do more harm. For example, children with autism frequently have smaller bones. Dairy products have nutrients that can strengthen their bones.

Many youngsters performed the same regardless of whether they ate meals containing casein, according to studies. Their autism symptoms did not decrease significantly. Some studies suggest that people with autism may have low amounts of key vitamins and minerals. This does not induce autism spectrum disease. However, your doctor may recommend supplements to boost your nutrition. Vitamin B and magnesium are two of the most commonly used supplements for people with autism.

However, humans can overdose on these vitamins, thus megavitamins should be avoided. However, some dietary adjustments may alleviate some autistic symptoms. Food allergies, for example, may exacerbate behavior difficulties. Removing the allergen from your child's diet may improve some behavioral concerns. The crucial thing is that your child's diet caters to their nutritional requirements and ASD symptoms. The best method to determine the most beneficial diet is to consult with your doctor and a nutrition consultant, such as a registered dietitian. They will assist you in creating a meal plan that is specifically tailored to your child. Some autistic children experience digestive issues such as constipation, stomach pain, nausea, and vomiting. Your doctor can recommend a diet that will not exacerbate these concerns.

Remember that nutritional needs alter over time. Your child's nutritionist will assist you ensure that the meals they eat continue to suit their needs as they grow older.

How to Help Your Child with Autism Communication To help your child with autism communicate more effectively, you can:

- Use their name so they know you're talking to them.
- Speak calmly and Keep the language clean and straightforward.
- Give them more time to understand what you just stated.
- Simple gestures, photos, or eye contact can assist children in understanding what you're saying.
- Avoid:Talking in a noisy or crowded environment Saying things with several meanings, such as "break a leg"
- Asking your child many questions.

Problems sleeping

Many children with autism have trouble falling or staying asleep.

You can assist them with:

- Maintaining a sleep diary to identify common difficulties
- Following the same bedtime ritual every night.
- Allowing them to sleep with earplugs, if that helps.
- Keeping their bedrooms dark and silent.
- Speaking with a doctor about conditions that may impact their sleep.

Socializing

To help your child establish friends and socialize, ask their school for assistance.

- Ask your autism care team for advice.
- Look through the National Autism Society database to find local social groups that can support people with autism.
- Request or read information from other parents of children with autism.
- Avoid forcing your child to participate in social activities if they prefer to be alone.
- Allow them time to gain social skills.

CHAPTER 2

Early Intervention And Therapy

Early intervention and therapy are crucial in promoting the development of children with autism. The early years of a child's life are characterized by fast brain growth, making timely and suitable interventions very effective.

This section discusses the necessity of early intervention, the numerous types of therapies available, and practical strategies for developing a successful therapy plan that is suited to each child's requirements.

Importance of Early Intervention

1. Early childhood is a critical era for brain development, and interventions can have long-term impacts.

Early intervention can improve cognitive, social, and behavioral outcomes by addressing developmental deficiencies and capitalizing on the brain's plasticity.

2. Improved Long-Term Outcomes: Early intervention helps children acquire daily living, communication, and social skills.- Early interventions can lower the severity of symptoms and the need for specialized care later in life.

3. Family Support: Early intervention programs provide support and training for families to better understand their child's needs and address them effectively. Empowering families with information and skills can help to reduce stress and enhance family dynamics.

Types of Therapies

1. Applied Behavioral Analysis (ABA): ABA is a widely used, evidence-based strategy that focuses on improving specific behaviors such as communication, social skills, and adaptive learning.

Techniques: Positive reinforcement, task analysis, and discrete trial training are among the techniques used.

Benefits: ABA is highly personalized and adaptable to a range of contexts, including the home, school, and community.

2. Speech therapy: Speech therapy tackles communication impairments, including both verbal and nonverbal communication.

Techniques: Techniques may include language development, articulation practice, and the use of alternate communication modalities such as sign language or communication equipment.

Benefits: Improves a child's capacity to express needs, interact socially, and absorb language.

3. Occupational Therapy (OT): Occupational therapy (OT) assists children in developing everyday living skills such as dressing, eating, and fine motor tasks.

Techniques include sensory integration therapy, motor skill improvement, and daily activity adaptation strategies.

Benefits: Enhances independence, coordination, and sensory processing.

4. Physical Therapy (PT): Physical therapy focuses on increasing gross motor skills, coordination, and strength.

Techniques: Exercises are used to improve balance, posture, and mobility.

Benefits: Promotes physical growth, lowers physical limits, and increases involvement in physical activities.

5. Social Skills Training: Social skills training teaches youngsters how to behave appropriately with peers and adults.

Techniques: Role-playing, social tales, and group activities are among the techniques used.

Benefits: Promotes a better awareness of social cues, strengthens peer relationships, and increases social participation.

6. Developmental and play-based therapies: Therapies such as the Developmental, Individual Differences, Relationship-based (DIR)/Floortime approach emphasize creating relationships and supporting emotional and social growth via play.

Techniques: The techniques include child-led play, engaging activities, and responsive interactions.

Benefits: Promotes emotional regulation, involvement, and social bonds.

Developing an Effective Therapy Plan

1. Assessment and Goal Setting: Initial Assessment: Conduct extensive assessments to better understand the child's strengths, challenges, and special requirements. This could include standardized testing, observations, and feedback from diverse professions.

Setting Goals. Using the assessment results, set clear, quantifiable, and achievable goals. Goals should be tailored to the child's developmental stage and individual needs.

2. Individualized Education Plans (IEPs). IEP Development: For school-aged children, collaborate with the educational team to create an Individualized Education Plan (IEP) outlining particular educational and therapeutic objectives.

Components of an IEP. The IEP should include explicit objectives, the sorts of services the child will receive, their frequency and duration, and how progress will be measured.

3. Collaboration with Professionals.
Team Approach: Work with a group of specialists, such as therapists, educators, and medical providers, to ensure a comprehensive approach to the child's development.

Regular Communication: Maintain open and continual communication with all team members to track progress, make changes, and guarantee consistency across settings.

4. Family involvement: Training and Support: Provide parents and caregivers with training and resources to help their children develop at home. This could include tactics for reinforcing skills, controlling behaviors, and fostering a supportive environment.

Involvement in Therapy: Encourage family members to attend therapy sessions and activities to guarantee skill continuity and reinforcement.

5. Progress Monitoring and Plan Adjustment.

Regular Reviews: Regularly examine and assess the child's progress toward their goals. This may include formal assessments, observations, and input from the child and family.

Adjusting Plans: Adjust the therapy plan based on progress and new information to ensure that it meets the child's changing needs and problems.

Early intervention and therapy are critical for helping children with autism acquire essential abilities and reach their full potential. By addressing developmental difficulties early and delivering personalized, evidence-based interventions, we can greatly improve long-term outcomes for children on the autistic spectrum.

Effective early intervention necessitates a collaborative, tailored strategy that includes professionals, family, and the child, all working together to foster a supportive and empowering environment. Early and continuous support can help children with autism lay a solid foundation for lifelong growth and achievement.

CHAPTER 3

Education And Schooling For People With Autism

Education is an important part of the development of children with autism since it provides opportunities for social contact, communication, and behavioral progress in addition to academic understanding. The educational demands of children with autism might vary greatly, demanding specialized approaches and support structures to ensure each child's success.

This section looks at the various educational settings, the significance and creation of Individualized Education Programs (IEPs), and strategies for fostering inclusive and supportive learning environments.

Choosing the appropriate educational setting

1. Mainstream/Inclusion Settings: In these environments, children with autism attend lessons alongside their neurotypical peers.

Benefits: Promotes social integration, introduces youngsters to a typical peer group, and helps develop acceptance and understanding among all students.

Considerations: Individual needs must be addressed within the wider classroom environment with proper support, such as aids or special education teachers.

2. Specialized Schools: These schools are specifically created for students with autism and other developmental problems.

Benefits: Creates a personalized atmosphere with specialized teaching methods, lower class sizes, and staff education in autism-specific practices.

Considerations: While these institutions provide substantial support, they may limit interactions with neurotypical students.

3. Hybrid models: Integrates features of both mainstream and specialized settings, frequently through part-time

inclusion in general education courses and part-time instruction in specialized settings.

Benefits: It strikes a balance between the requirement for specialist support and chances for social inclusion.

Considerations: General education and special education professionals must work closely together and communicate well.

4. Homeschooling: Parents are mostly responsible for their children's education, frequently employing individualized curriculum and flexible scheduling.

Benefits: Highly customized, adaptable to the child's pace and interests, and provides a controlled atmosphere.

Considerations: Parents must devote significant time, effort, and resources to guaranteeing their children's access to socialization activities.

Individualized education plans (IEPs)
1. Development of the IEP.- Assessment and Evaluation: Comprehensive examinations are carried out to identify the child's strengths, challenges, and unique requirements. This encompasses intellectual, social, behavioral, and communicative evaluations.

IEP Team: Includes parents, teachers, special education professionals, therapists, and other pertinent stakeholders. Collaboration ensures that the IEP represents the child's individual needs.

Goal Setting: Goals should be specific, measurable, attainable, relevant, and time-bound (SMART). They should cover not only academic skills but also social, behavioral, and functional needs.

2. IEP Components: Present Levels of Performance: Describes the child's present strengths and challenges across many domains.

Annual Goals: Clearly stated goals that the youngster is expected to meet within a year.

Special Education and Related Services: Describes the precise treatments that the kid will get, such as speech therapy, occupational therapy, or behavioral assistance.

Accommodations and Modifications: Changes to the curriculum, teaching methods, or surroundings that enable the child to learn more effectively.

Progress Monitoring: Methods and deadlines for assessing and reporting on the child's progress toward IEP goals.

3. Implementation and Review: Ongoing Monitoring: Regularly monitor and document the child's progress toward their IEP objectives. Adapt instructional tactics and supports depending on data and observations.

Annual Reviews: Hold formal IEP meetings at least once a year to examine the child's progress, update goals, and make any required changes to the IEP.

Parental Involvement: Encourage parents to actively participate in the IEP process. Maintain open communication to keep them informed and active in decision-making.

Inclusion versus Specialized Settings

1. Benefits of Inclusion: Social Interaction: Allows children with autism to interact with neurotypical peers, which can help them improve their social skills and relationships.

Diversity and Acceptance: Promotes a culture of diversity and inclusiveness among the school community.

Access to General Curriculum: Allows children with autism to participate in the same curriculum as their peers, with the necessary supports and modifications.

2. Challenges to Inclusion.
Need for Support: Teachers and staff must receive extensive support and training to effectively include children with autism in general education settings.

Isolation Potential: Without proper help, autistic children may feel alienated or fail to meet the demands of the normal classroom.

3. Advantages of Specialized Settings: targeted training: Offers individualized training targeted to the specific needs of children with autism.

Specialized Staff: Staff are often trained on autism-specific teaching tactics and interventions.

Focused Environment: Smaller class numbers and more regulated surroundings can help to prevent sensory overload and behavioral difficulties.

4. Difficulties in Specialized Settings.
Limited Social Interaction: This may hinder interactions with neurotypical classmates.

Stigma: This can lead to stigmatization or separation of autistic children from their mainstream peers.

Strategies for Effective Education

1. Creating a Supportive Learning Environment.

Structured Routine: Create a consistent daily routine to increase predictability and reduce anxiety.

Visual Supports: Visual calendars, prompts, and clocks can assist toddlers grasp expectations and transitions.

Sensory Accommodations: Create sensory-friendly surroundings that include sensory breaks and adjustments to lighting, noise, and seating arrangements. 2. Behavioral Interventions: Positive Reinforcement: Use positive reinforcement to promote desirable behaviors and skills.

Functional Behavior Assessments (FBA):. Conduct FBAs to better understand the causes of problematic behaviors and establish effective intervention programs.

Behavioral Plans: Use tailored behavior intervention plans (BIPs) to establish specific tactics and support for managing behaviors.

3. Social Skills Training: Peer Mediated Instruction: Prepare neurotypical peers to facilitate social connections and demonstrate acceptable behavior.

Social Stories and Role-Playing: Use social storytelling and role-playing games to teach social skills and how to respond appropriately in social situations.

Group Activities: Encourage involvement in group activities and joint projects to improve social skills and peer connections.

4. Communication strategies: Augmentative and Alternative Communication (AAC): Provide AAC devices or communication boards for children who are nonverbal or have limited speech.

Speech Therapy Integration: Integrate speech therapy goals and practices into the educational environment.

Consistent Communication Systems: Maintain consistency in communication strategies across several environments (home, school, therapy).

5. Parental involvement and advocacy: Home-School Collaboration: Encourage open communication and collaboration between home and school to help the kid develop and resolve any concerns.

Parent Training: Provide parents with training and resources to help them reinforce their learning and behavioral techniques at home.

Advocacy: Empower parents to advocate for their children's needs and rights in the educational system. Education and education are critical components of the developmental process for children with autism.

Educators and parents can build a supportive and empowered learning environment by selecting a suitable educational setting, developing and implementing effective IEPs, and employing evidence-based techniques. This method not only addresses academic needs but also supports social, communication, and behavioral growth, allowing children with autism to attain their full potential and thrive both inside and outside of the classroom.

CHAPTER 4

How To Support Someone With Autism

Autism changes how a person communicates, interacts with others, and perceives the environment. Some people with autism can live independently, while others require constant care and support to live fulfilling lives.

Understanding Autism

To provide the best possible support to the individuals in your life who have autism, you need first learn about the illness. Autism is a lifelong developmental disorder that affects how people communicate and interact with their environment.

Autism is distinguished by social communication difficulties, repetitive behaviors, and sensory sensitivities. People with autism frequently have difficulty interpreting traditional forms of verbal and nonverbal expression, such as gestures or tone of voice.

This can lead to difficulties in socializing or expressing their needs and desires. People with autism often find the world bewildering and overwhelming. This is why they frequently like rigidity and routine. Changes in habits or new, large events can be distressing for persons with autism and elicit negative emotions such as anxiety and panic.

Many persons with autism utilize repeated movements, such as rocking back and forth or flapping their hands, as a kind of comfort or enjoyment. Autism can lead people to be over or under-sensitive to specific sensory inputs such as taste, touch, smell, light, temperature, or sound. Something as basic as background music in a restaurant, which may irritate some, might be particularly unpleasant or disturbing for someone with autism.

It is critical to challenge common myths and preconceptions concerning autism. It is a prevalent misconception that persons with autism do not like to socialize or establish friends. Just because autism makes it difficult to socialize does not mean that people do not want to. They merely require positive reinforcement to boost their confidence, encourage independence, and foster pleasant social interactions.

Tips to Support Someone with Autism

When assisting someone with autism, remember the golden rule: never make assumptions. Before doing anything for the person, always ask them about their preferred communication method. For example, before closing a window in their room or residence, ask them if they want you to do so. The finest assistance is one that encourages the individual to live a life of independence and personal choice.

How to Communicate with People with Autism:

- Use straightforward wording.
- Try to be concise and straightforward.
- Avoid using metaphorical language or any other terminology that could be misinterpreted or taken literally.
- Use Visual Aids: Some people with autism benefit greatly from visual assistance.
- Try using visuals, symbols, or textual instructions to help the person grasp what you're saying. Visual calendars, social stories, and visual cue cards can be especially useful.
- Allow time for processing: People with autism may require additional time to process information and consider their responses.
- Be patient and don't rush or disrupt their thinking.

- Be aware of sensory sensitivity: Some people with autism may have sensory sensitivities, which can interfere with communication.
- Pay attention to their surroundings and avoid distractions or overwhelming sensory inputs that may make it difficult for them to focus.
- Creating a calm and sensory-friendly environment helps improve engagement.
- Focus on your abilities and interests: Find shared hobbies to utilize as conversation starters. People with autism frequently have specific areas of interest or skill.
- Use these themes to get kids interested in communicating and expressing their passions.
- Be patient and nonjudgmental. Anyone would find it difficult not to be allowed to express themselves freely. When speaking to someone with autism, be patient and empathetic, and be open to changing your approach to match their requirements.
- Utilize technology and alternative communication channels. Augmentative and alternative communication (AAC) solutions, such as communication applications or photo exchange systems, can assist those with limited verbal communication abilities.
- Explore and use these resources. Help them develop daily living skills. Be aware of sensory

sensitivities. Individuals with autism frequently exhibit sensory sensitivities, such as increased sensitivity to noise, touch, or particular textures. Everyday sounds that others find tolerable can be overwhelming, and some textures or tactile sensations can be uncomfortable or distressing.

Understanding and addressing these sensory sensitivities can significantly improve the comfort and well-being of people with autism.

- **Here are some strategies to support sensory sensitivities:** Reduce the noise levels: To reduce background noise, use sound-absorbing materials, close windows, or use white noise machines. Offer noise-canceling headphones or earplugs as an alternative for those who are sensitive to noise.

- Optimize lighting: Use natural light if possible and adjust artificial lighting to reduce glare or harshness. Avoid flickering lights and instead use dimmer switches or softer lighting solutions. Provide sensory breaks and calm areas. Create a peaceful and quiet location where people can retreat when they are feeling overwhelmed. Fill the space with soothing materials such as bean bags, weighted blankets, and fidget toys.

- Consider the visual elements: Create a visually organized, clutter-free environment. Avoid excessive visual stimuli, such as bright colors or busy patterns.

- Provide sensory tools and materials: Allow access to sensory tools such as stress balls, textured objects, and chewable items. These can help people control their sensory input and cope with worry or stress.

To accommodate tactile sensitivity, provide a variety of soft, tagless, and comfortable clothing options. Respect people's particular touch preferences and allow them to determine how much physical contact they are comfortable with. Be careful of fragrances. Use unscented or mildly scented cleaning solutions, and avoid using strong smells in the environment. Maintain adequate ventilation to reduce smells.

Supporting Social Interactions
Many people with autism like socializing and making new acquaintances; they only want positive reinforcement to make the most of their social lives. Some people with autism have limited speech or language skills, whereas others have excellent language skills but struggle to understand sarcasm or interpret social cues.

Use these suggestions to encourage positive social relationships with our loved ones:

- Offer structured social opportunities.
- Encourage engagement in social activities or groups that correspond to the individual's interests. This provides a friendly and structured environment in which they may interact with their classmates and practice their social skills.
- Encourage children and peers to be understanding, patient, and inclusive when playing and doing activities together. This benefits everyone by instilling a sense of inclusion and belonging. Implement social skills practice. To educate and practice social skills, employ tactics such as role-playing, social storytelling, and video modeling.
- Give plenty of positive praise and feedback. This can help people better perceive social cues and handle social situations with less fear.
- Use visual supports: Visual tools, such as social scripts or visual calendars, can help people with autism comprehend social expectations. Visual aids provide a basic portrayal of social standards, making them easier to grasp and apply.
- Create clear expectations: Make social expectations obvious and unambiguous, breaking them down into manageable steps. Use clear and detailed language to help autistic persons

understand what is expected of them in various social contexts.

- Collaborate with professional and support networks. Collaborate with therapists, educators, and support workers to create socialization tactics that are specific to each individual.

Advice to Support Networks and Caregivers

It is critical that you look after yourself. If you are fatigued or overwhelmed, you will be unable to provide the necessary support.

Here are some suggestions for prioritizing self-care and scheduling time for yourself to refuel and rejuvenate:

- Make Time for Yourself: Schedule regular breaks or respite care to give you time to focus on your health.
- Engage in activities that make you happy and help you relax, such as hobbies, exercise, or spending time with loved ones.
- Allow yourself to take breaks from caregiving by assigning responsibilities to trusted others such as family members, friends, or respite care providers.
- Seek help. Reach out to support groups or internet communities. You will be able to connect

with other caregivers who share your experiences. Don't be afraid to seek support from family, friends, or professionals. Accepting help can relieve some of the burden of caregiving.

- Use stress management techniques: Deep breathing exercises, mindfulness, and meditation are all stress-management practices that you can learn and practice. Find healthy stress relief activities, such as journaling, hobbies, or listening to relaxing music.

Consider obtaining professional support, such as therapy or counseling. A therapist can offer advice, coping skills, and a secure environment in which to process your feelings and problems as a caregiver

Best Communication Practices for Interacting with Autistic People

Ways to Develop Relationships and Rapport

- Be patient throughout a conversation, giving the person time to respond. Always aim to be encouraging and empathetic.
- Learn about their favorite interests, activities, and hobbies, and try to identify common ones.
- Be aware that autistic persons tend to speak at length about their preferred topics, which may necessitate some gentle urging or redirection.

Maintaining communication can also be difficult. You can help them by providing options, suggesting themes, or directing the conversation to a topic you know they can discuss. Provide simple instructions or clear options. For example, "Would you like to go for a walk or ride our bikes?" Provide specific praise, such as "I liked the way you waited for me before leaving the room," rather than a general "good job," so kids understand what conduct you want from them. To make your communication clearer, tell the individual what you want them to do rather than what you don't want them to do. For example, instead of saying "Don't run," say "Please walk in the hall." Do not be offended by a lack of eye contact, motor tics, or a failure to recognize personal boundaries. These are typical obstacles for autistic people. Understand that autistic persons enjoy routines and schedules. Autistic people think literally and, therefore, avoid idioms and slang.

Pointers to assist autistic persons if they get off track or spend too much time on a topic:

A gentle nudge or prompt to get back on track, such as "What were we talking about again?" Or refocus them by bringing up the original topic of discussion, such as "Where should we go for lunch?" You seem to enjoy Chinese food; how about the XYZ establishment at 11:45 a.m.?" (Ideally, avoid noisy or crowded areas)"To summarize, our next actions are XYZ, with your portion being this and due by x date. Does it seem to cover all we discussed?" In a gentle yet specific manner, such as "I hear you like talking about dinosaurs, But I'm not interested in that and don't want to talk about it any longer; can we talk about something we both care about?" Then propose something you have in common or may share, such as a favorite movie or meal.

Boundary issues

Social communication might be difficult for autistic individuals. They may have varied perspectives on areas of social norms for various types of people. For example, realize that a teacher or supervisor is not the same as a social friend. Or the distinction between a friend and a friendly acquaintance.

They may not comprehend how much personal space to give people. Autistic persons are more literal, so offering gentle but direct guidance in a friendly tone can be beneficial. If you want to assist someone with boundary issues: If they appear to be standing too near to you, be gentle but direct. For example, you could say, "Could you kindly stand approximately this distance away from me when we're talking? Thank you very much. (Raise your arm slightly to indicate how far apart you mean.)

If the individual touches your hair, hugs you improperly, or engages in other physical interactions, you can begin by moving aside and out of reach. If the behavior is persistent or irritating, ask the offender to cease. You might also distract them by focusing their attention on something else, such as an activity. You can also demonstrate the physical distance and suitable placement of your own hands at your sides, in your pocket, arms folded, and so on.

If the individual shares personal information with you that you are uncomfortable with since you are not a friend or close to them, try to shift the conversation to something more acceptable. If that doesn't work, you can politely inform them that the matter is too personal.

Communication Style

Provide options for how the person wishes to interact, such as texting, phone calls, emailing, or in-person conversations.

Don't assume that everyone wants to communicate in the same way.

Making the objective or reason for communication apparent (e.g., in college, is it a social or class project) assists the autistic person in preparing and setting expectations.

Autistic persons thrive in environments with organization and clarity. However, it does not have to be official. An agenda is not required; simply share the topic, such as, "We're going to meet to plan logistics for a specific event." Be mindful that some persons have limited communication abilities or preferences, and may require nonverbal approaches such as visual timetables, tablets, pointing, or picture exchange systems.

Managing Sensory

Issues Autistic people may experience greater sensory issues with touch, sound, light, smell, and taste than neurotypical people. Consider the loud sounds, bright lights, strong odors, and dietary concerns that your autistic friend or colleague may find most difficult.

Consider how to address the needs of others during meetings or business contacts. For example, avoid restaurants or meeting places that offer intensive sensory stimulation. Choose a peaceful, uncluttered area to reduce distractions, which may also help your team focus more effectively. You may think of it as delivering relaxing, serene, and zen/meditation-like environments as opposed to gamified colorful, brilliant, and dynamic settings.

When overstimulated, an autistic person may utilize a variety of self-soothing tactics, including leaving the room or region to avoid a breakdown or shutdown. Alternatively, they may simply struggle to focus and perform at their best. Consider creating sensory-friendly meeting locations or classrooms, such as subdued lights, comfortable chairs, limited distractions in the room, and neutral colors.

For Those Who Are More Affected on the Spectrum, Nonverbal, or Require Extra Assistance People who are more impacted will have more needs in areas such as communication and sensory difficulties, as well as require more extensive assistance in everyday functioning.

Nonverbal communication, on the other hand, does not always imply greater impact. Don't make assumptions about a person's intellectual level based on their low or nonverbal communication skills. After giving directions, pause to allow the person to process the verbal information. Offer to provide simple written instructions or a checklist for typical or unusual tasks.

Give the person options during the conversation (for example, "Would you like a sandwich or pizza?").

When possible, questions should be written so that they only present acceptable options. For instance, if a manager inquires, "Would you like to join us for this meeting?" An autistic person may respond by saying "no" and returning to their workstation. This is because a command is being phrased as a question. In this situation, instead say, "Please join us for a meeting in the conference room at 10:00 a.m." (You may need to come to fetch them depending on their degree of functioning.) Have the recipient repeat crucial information to ensure knowledge (for example, after sharing that information, ask, "Where are we going?").

Use photos or drawings to help the person communicate (for example, images of food or activity options). Visual timetables, in which you use a photo or image to represent the activities planned, can also be useful. Although some people can hold hours-long talks, others may only be able to answer a single question or participate in a conversation for 5 minutes. In these instances, providing pauses for the individual can be beneficial in keeping them calmer and more focused. If someone is nonverbal Inquire about the person's or caregiver's preferred mode of communication.

Learn about the assistance devices and tactics they may utilize. For example, visual schedules, iPad apps, text-to-speech, and other voice assistant apps in which a user touches something on their device to talk to them.

Always gaze at the person you're attempting to speak with, not their caretaker.

If you were employing a translator for someone who spoke a foreign language, you would focus on the person you wanted to communicate with rather than the interpreter.

Use gestures in addition to spoken communication.

Allow ample time for people using assistive devices to type their comments.

Do not talk about them in front of them as if they are not present.

Always face them when speaking with them, even if they don't appear to be paying attention.

Always communicate what you're doing, even if you don't think they understand.

How to be a friend to a person with ASD
The greatest method to be supportive and build a positive relationship with someone is to ask how you can be a good friend, coworker, and so on.

Do not be hesitant to ask your autistic friend, "How can I be a better friend?" When spending time with an autistic friend, pay attention and don't rush to respond.

Simply listen: You might have to wait longer for an answer or sift through a lengthy explanation, but you will learn something new in the end. If a friend seeks assistance, offer your support. Consider what they want and need, rather than how you think they should improve or behave.

Try not to talk over or about them when others are present.

Help them develop social skills by engaging them in conversations with you and others.

Find discreet ways to drop social cues.

Build their confidence in the same manner that you would help any other buddy in a difficult situation. Try not to intervene and make decisions for your companion in a social environment.

It's crucial to plan when you'll meet with a friend. Preventing uncomfortable circumstances is significantly easier than dealing with them after they occur. Instead of going to your favorite brunch restaurant at 11:00 a.m. on a Sunday, consider arriving after the rush at 2:00 p.m. Alternatively, if you know there will be a big line or wait somewhere, go early (or late) to escape the crowds.

CHAPTER 5

Teaching Independent Living Skills

Most people want to be able to live independently, especially as they get older. People with intellectual disabilities and other disorders, such as autism spectrum disorder, frequently wish to live as independently as possible, as do their parents and caregivers. Although some children on the autism spectrum may never be able to live independently, parents frequently hope that their children will learn as much as they can about daily living skills such as caring for their bodies, performing basic household chores, preparing their meals or snacks, and cleaning up after themselves.

Supporting Independent Living for Children and Young Adults with Autism
There are a few things you can do to help your kid or adult with autism succeed in independent living. The individual you are assisting should be able to do the following:

Recognize, appraise, and prioritize his or her interests, abilities, and essential requirements. Know his abilities. Recognize and express his interests, values, and views. When teaching independent living skills to people with autism, start by helping them discover their specific interests, abilities, and requirements, as well as their preferences, values, and beliefs. These will help students prepare for independent life in both their current and future situations.

Consider how a person who self-reflects and is aware of their own needs, abilities, and preferences might better choose a career that fits their personality. Can they access and participate in fun activities? Does employment demand them to interact with a large number of people? Is the employment in a noisy place, or can it be done from the confines of their home? These types of questions can assist persons on the spectrum in determining the best job path for themselves.

Important Skills for Independent Living
Independent living is a broad term that encompasses a number of distinct abilities. Some of the abilities that a kid (or an adult) with autism should learn to encourage an independent life include Decision-making Self-assessment (assessing one's conduct and the repercussions of such activities) Communication Self-care skills.

Social skills Basic academic skills (including reading, writing, and mathematics) Self-management Community functioning work-related skills. Basic daily living abilities.

Some of the essential daily living skills that can be taught when assisting your child with independent living include cooking, cleaning up after oneself, money management, domestic duties, shopping, and accessing transportation. It's also critical to teach your child executive functioning abilities, which are related to how they think and process information. You may educate your child on executive functioning skills such as organizing, planning, and time management.

Core Independent Living Skills
One study looked at the perspectives of people with disabilities, their caregivers, and the professionals who work with them. The study aimed to determine what these groups believe are the most significant qualities of a person's capacity to live independently.

The findings of that investigation were as follows: Professionals believed that individuals with intellectual disabilities should be taught everyday living skills to live independently, as well as self-care skills and understanding of security laws. Parents also believed that daily living skills, awareness of security standards, and understanding of self-care should be prioritized to encourage their child's independence. Individuals with disabilities stated that the most important things they need to know to live independently are financial management and professional work skills.

These findings suggest that if we want to assist children and adults with autism to live independently, we should focus on daily living skills as well as career and money management abilities. Learning these can be useful whether the person lives alone, with a roommate, or with their parents.

Tips for Teaching Independent Living Skills to Children with Autism

1. Customize Your Teaching Approach. Every individual is unique, including those on the autism spectrum. When it comes to promoting independent living, the skills you should focus on will depend on your child's specific requirements, abilities, objectives for themselves, and goals for you. Individualize your teaching method based on what works best for your youngster.

2. Structured Versus Natural Approach When teaching independent living skills to a kid with autism, you can use a structured or formal method, a more natural and flexible approach, or a combination of the two. To teach

your child a skill in a systematic fashion, have him practice verbally telling you the steps to constructing a snack (such as a peanut butter and jelly sandwich) or placing the stages in order when you show him images or phrases that represent the processes. Teaching naturally entails having your child make the sandwich for a snack.

3. Evaluate Your Child's Current Skills It is beneficial to analyze your child's existing ability in specific skills. Observe your child and make a note of what they do well and what they struggle with. Alternatively, look at a specific ability and decide which element of it your child needs more help with. You can also consider receiving a formal assessment from a Board-Certified Behavior Analyst (BCBA), who can evaluate your child's current level of functioning and identify areas where he or she could improve.

4. Visual Supports Visual aids are an excellent approach to educating children with autism new abilities. They can provide visual cues or assistance to the youngsters to help them accomplish specific tasks more freely and effectively. Checklists, calendars, pictorial schedules, color coding systems, charts, lists, and token boards are examples of such tools.

5. Other Resources to Help Your Child Using technology can also assist your youngster develop independent living skills. For example, if they have a smartphone, you may assist them with setting alarms to remind them of specific activities or teaching them how to use their phone's calendar.

6. Practice, Practice, Practice! Independence is not easy for anyone. Daily living skills, self-care skills, and other critical skills that promote independent living require extensive practice for the majority of people, including those without impairments. Encourage and support your youngster, and understand that developing independence will take time.

It is also important that you help your child practice the skills you are working on in a variety of ways. For example, if your child is learning how to count and spend money, you can practice with play money during playtime, or you might set up a "store" at home and have your child earn money to spend on store things. Also, make sure your child has real-world opportunities to practice this in the community.

7. Establishing Routines Routines are an important method for supporting independent living. You can help your child by demonstrating daily routines. Establish routines that you follow on your own or with your child.

You can assist your child in developing daily routines for chores that are vital in their daily lives. You can provide visual assistance, such as a checklist, to help them become more independent in following daily routines.

Community-Based Skills Assessment Independent life includes community-based skills. Autism Speaks has a tool called the Community-Based Skills Assessment, which parents and clinicians can use to evaluate a person's abilities in several areas. The assessment is intended for children aged 12 and up.

Remember, there is no "one-size-fits-all" approach to teaching independent living skills. When making this decision, keep your child's specific needs and talents in mind. You have got this!

CHAPTER 6

Empowering Autistic People: Developing Life Skills For Independence

Life is a journey full of difficulties and opportunities, and for those on the autism spectrum, learning basic life skills is critical to gaining independence and a satisfying life.

Understanding Autism and Life Skills. Autism is a neurodevelopmental condition that alters how people perceive and interact with the world. While autism manifests itself differently for each individual, there are certain common issues that many people confront. One of the most difficult aspects of autism for autistic people is learning to live alone.

These skills, which include both basic and complicated tasks, are critical for gaining independence and self-confidence. Daily Life Skills for Autism Autism includes the following daily living skills:

- Communication Skills: Effective communication is an essential component of daily life. Autistic people may require specific assistance in developing their verbal and nonverbal communication skills. Speech therapy, social skills training, and assistive communication equipment can be quite beneficial in this situation.
- Self-care Skills: Basic personal hygiene and self-care rituals, such as washing, clothing, and grooming, are critical for sustaining physical health and well-being. Autistic adults may require direction and support in these areas to ensure their independence.
- Time Management: The ability to manage time properly is essential for independent living. Learning to plan, prioritize, and stick to a schedule can significantly improve a person's capacity to live an organized life.
- Money Management: Financial freedom is an important component of adult life. Individuals with autism can benefit from learning budgeting, banking, and financial planning through specialized support and education.

- Cooking and nutrition: Knowing how to prepare meals and make healthy food choices is vital for daily life. Cooking lessons and nutrition instruction can help autistic adults make healthier eating choices. Autistic Life Skills Activities

- Social Skills Workshops: Autistic people frequently struggle in social situations. Participating in autistic social skills courses helps teach them how to start conversations, create friends, and recognize social cues. Occupational therapy can assist autistic persons improve their fine motor skills and sensory processing abilities. This therapy can help them accomplish everyday duties more effectively. Independent Autism

- Living Skills Programs: Many organizations provide independent Autism living skills workshops that are tailored to the needs of autistic adults. These programs teach a variety of skills, including housekeeping, time management, and vocational training.

- Vocational Training: Preparing for a job is an important component of independent living. Individuals on the autistic spectrum can benefit from vocational training programs that teach them job-relevant skills.

Autism and Independent

Living Skills Living Arrangements: Autistic persons can live independently, with family, or in supported living arrangements. The choice is based on their ability and personal preferences. All of these solutions require autism-specific independent living abilities.

Transportation: Learning how to use public transportation or drive a car is a valuable life skill that can lead to more independence and job prospects.

Health and Safety: Understanding fundamental health and safety precautions is critical. Autistic people should be prepared to manage emergencies and seek medical attention when necessary.

Emotional and Psychological Wellbeing Developing life skills involves not only practical duties but also emotional and psychological well-being. When faced with daily challenges, autistic people may feel more stressed and anxious. It is critical to provide emotional support while also fostering a safe and inclusive environment.

Encouraging self-advocacy, self-esteem, and self-regulation skills can help people with autism better manage their emotions and mental health.

A holistic approach. A comprehensive strategy is required when developing living skills for autistic adults. This includes taking into account each person's specific requirements and strengths. Autism is a highly variable disorder, therefore a one-size-fits-all strategy may be ineffective.

Assessments and personalized plans can assist autistic people in developing the precise life skills they require while also utilizing their strengths and interests.

The Function of Families and Support Networks
Families, friends, and support networks play an important role in helping autistic people learn and develop life skills. They can offer support, guidance, and practical assistance as needed.

Furthermore, support groups and communities can be quite useful for sharing experiences and learning from one another. Nurturing life skills in autistic individuals is more than just cultivating independence; it is also about promoting inclusion and increasing their general quality of life.

Recognizing the importance of daily living skills for autism and supporting initiatives such as autism life skills activities and programs can help individuals on the autistic spectrum live satisfying, meaningful, and independent lives. Recognizing that everyone has distinct skills and needs is critical to building a more inclusive and accepting community. We must ensure that every person, regardless of neurodiversity, has the opportunity to grow and realize their full potential.

CHAPTER 7

Employment And Vocational Training For People With Autism

Employment and vocational training are critical for promoting independence and improving the quality of life for people with autism. While people with autism experience unique obstacles in the workplace, they often contribute essential abilities and insights. With the right assistance and training, people can succeed in a variety of job environments.

This section discusses the importance of employment, different vocational training programs, job placement and retention tactics, and how to create inclusive workplaces.

Importance of Employment

1. Independence and Self-Sufficiency: Employment promotes financial independence and decreases reliance

on family or government help. It instills a sense of independence and personal accomplishment.

2. Social Inclusion: Workplaces provide opportunities for individuals with autism to develop social skills and relationships.

Employment can help alleviate social isolation and improve community cohesion.

3. Skill Development: Employment and vocational training help individuals gain and refine abilities that are useful in and out of the workplace.

These abilities include communication, problem-solving, time management, and teamwork.

4. Enhanced Quality of Life.Having a job can raise self-esteem, give you a feeling of purpose, and improve your general well-being.

It helps to establish an organized daily schedule, which is good for many people with autism.

Vocational Training Programs

1. Job coaching and supported employment: Provides one-on-one assistance to clients in learning job

responsibilities, understanding company culture, and navigating social interactions.

Benefits: Individualized support based on needs, with aid gradually reduced as the individual gains independence.

Implementation: Job coaches collaborate with both employees and employers to guarantee effective job placement and integration.

2. Pre-Employment Transition Services (Pre-ETS): Provides programs to high school students with disabilities to help them prepare for the transition from school to work.

The program's components include career exploration counseling, work-based learning experiences, post-secondary education counseling, workplace preparation training, and self-advocacy instruction.

Benefits: Assists students in identifying career interests, developing job-related skills, and gaining practical experience.

3. Vocational Rehabilitation (VR) Programs: State-funded programs that assist people with disabilities in preparing for, obtaining, and retaining employment.

Their services include career counseling, job training, resume development, interview preparation, job placement aid, and follow-up support.

Eligibility: Individuals must meet particular requirements for disability and employment barriers.

4. Apprenticeships and internships: Offer hands-on, practical experience in a real-world professional setting.

Benefits: Allow individuals to use their abilities in a supportive environment, obtain mentorship, and potentially advance to permanent employment.

Implementation: Partnerships among vocational training programs, employers, and educational institutions can help to make these opportunities more accessible.

5. Specialized Training Programs: Programs built expressly for people with autism, focused on improving abilities that match their strengths and interests.

Components: Training in technology, data entry, manufacturing, customer service, and other industries may be offered.

Benefits include tailored training and assistance that addresses the specific learning methods and requirements of people with autism.

Job placement and retention strategies

1. Assessment and Career Planning: Assessment of skills and interests. Conduct assessments to determine the individual's strengths, interests, and professional goals.

Personalized Career Plan: Create a detailed career plan that outlines short- and long-term work objectives, as well as the appropriate training and support requirements.

2. Job Matching: Fit with Strengths: Match job prospects to an individual's talents, interests, and strengths to boost job happiness and performance.

Work Environment Considerations: Consider sensory sensitivities and other environmental elements that could affect the individual's comfort and performance.

3. Interview Preparation: Mock Interviews: Conduct practice interviews to help the individual become comfortable with frequent interview questions and settings.

Social Stories and Role-Playing: Use social stories and role-playing to teach proper interview behaviors and replies.

Disclosure Strategies: Discuss the benefits and drawbacks of sharing an autism diagnosis with possible employers, and devise a strategy for disclosure if selected.

4. Workplace Accommodations: Determine and implement reasonable accommodations, such as flexible work schedules, reduced tasks, assistive technology, and quiet workspaces.

Sensory-Friendly Environment: Make improvements to alleviate sensory overload, such as giving noise-canceling headphones, altering lighting, or creating a peaceful location for breaks.

5. Job-site assistance.
Job Coaching: Offer job coaching to help individuals learn job responsibilities, navigate social interactions, and adapt to workplace culture.

Peer mentorship: Set up peer mentorship programs in which a coworker guides and supports the individual with autism.

6. Ongoing Training and Development.
Continuous Skill Development: Provide opportunities for continual training to assist individuals learn new skills and improve in their careers.

Feedback and Evaluation: Give the person regular comments and evaluations to help them understand their performance and areas for growth.

Creating Inclusive Workplaces

1. Employer Education and Training: Awareness Training: Conduct training workshops for companies and employees to raise awareness about autism and its strengths and problems.

Inclusion ways: Teach ways for fostering an inclusive and supportive work environment, such as good communication skills and accommodations.

2. Inclusive Hiring Practices:
Diverse Recruitment: Use recruitment strategies that actively aim to include people with impairments, including autism.

Interview Adjustments: Modify interview protocols to suit varied communication styles and lessen anxiety, such as permitting written responses or distributing interview questions ahead of time.

3. Positive Workplace Culture:
Acceptance and Respect: Create an inclusive company culture that encourages diversity, acceptance, and respect for all employees.

Team Building: Encourage team-building activities and social events that foster inclusiveness and understanding among all employees.

4. Policy Development:
Accommodation Policies: Create and enforce clear policies for requesting and providing accommodations.

Implement and implement strict anti-discrimination policies to protect employees with autism from bias and unfair treatment.

Employment and vocational training are critical components of a successful life for people with autism. We can develop pathways to meaningful and gratifying employment by identifying and resolving their specific obstacles, as well as maximizing their abilities. Individuals with autism can achieve professional success and more independence by participating in personalized vocational training programs, implementing effective job placement and retention techniques, and creating inclusive workplaces. This, in turn, broadens the workforce's variety and productivity, benefiting both people and society at large.

CHAPTER 8

Strategies To Manage Stress And Anxiety

Given the current status of the global health crisis, it is unsurprising that many of us are battling with our mental health as we experience increased stress and worry. This may be especially true for caregivers of people with special needs, as well as those of us who have underlying disorders that make dealing with stressful situations even more difficult.

It is now more important than ever to understand how to better equip ourselves to deal with stress and anxiety. Stress versus Anxiety It's worth noting that the terms stress and anxiety are frequently used interchangeably, even though they are two distinct ideas.

Stress is often the result of unexpected news, expectations, change, or uncertainty. When someone is distressed, they usually know what they are upset about. A cause can be identified, such as the pandemic, which has resulted in the need to homeschool or adjust to vocational and financial changes. Stress is frequently related to frustration and is always the outcome of an external force—something that creates outside pressure.

Anxiety stems from a state of internal uneasiness, characterized by fear and worry. Stressful events can cause anxiety, especially when a person is weary, dubious of their ability, has difficulty expressing their demands, or feels out of control. Unlike stress, it is often difficult to determine what is creating the anxious emotion.

When someone is anxious, their reaction to their emotions becomes part of the difficulty, such as anxiousness about an upcoming occasion. Anxiety is defined as expecting potential danger and having worried thoughts about how to face the event. Anxiety entails fear.

For example, a parent may feel anxious about an upcoming teacher conference. The parent may be concerned about a potential negative outcome for their child's future. This anxiety may result in increased worry, negative self-talk, or even the thinking of several worst-case scenarios—events that are unlikely to occur.

Anticipatory anxiety is the worry or dread that arises before an upcoming event. Anticipatory anxiety can range from mild anxiousness to crippling dread and cause circular thinking. People on the spectrum have stress and anxiety challenges.

Managing stress or anxiety can be difficult for some people on the autistic spectrum (and those with similar characteristics). This could be because coping tactics necessitate executive functioning skills and specialized cognitive reasoning abilities, such as recognizing symptoms, causality, and emotions, as well as memorizing relief measures.

Stress and anxiety also produce stress hormones. Many autistic people, including myself, endure anxiety and stress daily, with episodes of acute fear or panic. Some of us suffer from both Generalized Anxiety Disorder and Post-traumatic Stress Disorder.

An autistic person may respond in ways that are not immediately recognized as standard anxiety indicators. Some examples include withdrawal, meltdown, shutdown, repetitious speech or action, increased time spent on an interest or pastime, obsessive thoughts, or an insistence on or lack of routine.

Regardless of our neurology, numerous ways can help us and our loved ones cope during these moments of emotional distress.

The following is a list of ten strategies to reduce stress and anxiety.

1. Talk it out. Sharing sentiments with someone can often be the most effective way to decrease tension or worry. Talking things out (or writing them down in a journal) is frequently a wonderful method to reduce distress and worry. Consider creating a visual graph to identify occurrences that cause heightened worry. Engage in conversations to determine how stress and anxiety emerge in the body and actions.

2. Develop an emotional vocabulary. Teach and learn how to detect and recognize emotions. Label fundamental emotions (happy, sad, mad, disappointed, terrified, etc.), examine the degrees of different emotions, and make a list of complex emotions. Play emotional charades.

Paint or draw while listening to music and explore the emotions that arise. Create emotional sculptures out of dough. Create an emotive art pizza (gluten-free, as needed).

3. Track stresses. Determine which scenarios cause a significant level of uneasiness. Determine whether pressures are controlled, uncontrollable, or important/less important. Record thoughts, feelings, and facts about the surroundings, including the people and situations involved, as well as the physical setting and reactions. Taking notes might help with finding trends and answers.

4. Move through it. A brisk 20-minute stroll once or twice a day can be extremely beneficial to both the body and the mind. Establish moments for movement through dance or a type of moderate exercise. Stretches can be included in choreography. Extend the bend to pick up a piece of clothing off the floor. When you pick up your mail, take a walk around the block. Invest in roller skates or walking sticks. Walk to the corner grocery store. Play tag or "The Floor is Lava" in the house. Create an obstacle course in the backyard.

5. Immerse in nature. Simply placing your feet on the ground might help anchor emotions and introduce new perspectives. Engage with the outdoors. Leave nuts or seeds outside for birds to eat. Gather mushrooms for identification (do not consume). Take hikes among the trees. Nature can be brought indoors by growing plants from seed, adopting a pet, playing nature noises, or

utilizing essential oils. Try to watch inspiring nature documentaries. Create a Nature Week theme at home.

6. Recharge batteries. Breathe deeply several times during the day. Engage in prayer, mindfulness, or meditation. Find a peaceful area to listen to the birds or your favorite music. Make a music playlist. Play a game or unwind in another soothing activity, such as a warm shower or bubble bath. Drive around town to have some alone time without a destination in mind. Do something less serious and less deliberate. Escape into a captivating book or movie plot. Get a good night's sleep or nap. Treat yourself to something you enjoy. Take a staycation or check into a local place.

7. Nourish and drink. Nutrition can help you maintain good health. Eat something if you haven't eaten in a long time. Protein during breakfast is shown to reduce anxiety levels. Rehydrate. Keep note of your food and water intake. Consider studying foods and supplements that naturally relieve stress and anxiety. Explore a winery, outdoor garden, or farmer's market. Invest in a juicer. Consider a delivery service for fresh produce.

8. Manage time. Set aside time at the beginning of each day to prioritize chores. When feeling overwhelmed, consider making helpful and realistic ideas. Be realistic about what is possible under the conditions. Avoid

overcommitting. Avoid perfectionism. Set realistic expectations for yourself and others. If you are feeling pressured, evaluate your requirements and set boundaries and moments of rest. Block out hours on the calendar for stress management, hygiene maintenance, creative projects, calling friends, and productivity.

9. Give it time. Remember that some days will be harsher than others. Do not try to solve problems or debate while you are distressed or anxious. Allow time to process and regroup. Keep a slogan or encouraging phrases handy, and adjust your calendar as needed. Cancel appointments that may be delayed. Decide on the most important item to spend time on, then do it.

10. Use your best judgment. Try not to take any actions or comments personally, and instead assume good intentions over malice, ill will, or other negative assumptions. This includes being kind to oneself, allowing space to be human, and experiencing your own and others' emotions without shame.

Any signs of extreme emotions should be reported to a mental health expert or medical specialist, especially if they indicate a risk of self-harm or endangerment. Reach out and get help. Remember to take care of yourself.

CHAPTER 9

Benefits Of Autism Special Interests

Understanding Autism: Special Interests
Autism special interests are a distinct and valuable component of the autistic experience. They allude to the intense and focused interests that people with autism develop. In this section, we will look at what autism's special interests are and how they manifest in people on the autism spectrum.

What are Autism Special Interests?
Autism special interests are narrowly focused areas of interest or hobbies that fascinate people with autism. These interests frequently extend beyond traditional hobbies and can become an integral part of their lives.

Autism special interests can vary greatly from person to person and cover a wide range of things such as animals, trains, music, computers, and more.

Common Autism Special Interests: Animals trained in Music Computers Mathematics Astronomy Autism Special interests are typically passionate and all-encompassing, with people devoting significant time and energy to them. They enable people with autism to interact with the world, pursue their passions, and find joy and fulfillment.

How Do Special Interests Show Up in Autism?
Special interests in autism can emerge in a variety of ways, depending on the person.

Some common qualities are: Individuals with autism may have an amazing capacity to concentrate and focus on a specific interest for long periods.

- Broad information: They gain in-depth and broad information about their unique interest, frequently becoming specialists in their chosen field.

- Repetitive Behaviors: Engaging in repetitive activities connected to their unique interest, such as collecting stuff, organizing information, or performing certain rituals.

- Sensory Engagement: Many people with autism use their specific interests to connect with the world through their senses. For example, a special interest in music could entail listening to and evaluating various genres or playing musical instruments.

- Emotional Connection: People with autism frequently find comfort, familiarity, and emotional connection in their special interests. They can bring you joy, relaxation, and freedom to express yourself.

Understanding and understanding autism's unique interests is critical to creating a friendly and inclusive environment for those on the autism spectrum.

Recognizing the relevance of these interests allows us to support and foster the particular abilities and talents of people with autism, thus improving their general well-being and quality of life.

Accepting the Uniqueness of Autism Special Interests
Autism special interests are an important part of a person's life on the autism spectrum. Understanding and accepting these distinct interests allows parents to provide support and build an environment that promotes growth and development.

In this section, we will look at the benefits of recognizing and encouraging autism's unique interests.

Recognize the positive impact

Recognizing the beneficial influence of autism special interests is critical for comprehending their importance. Individuals on the autistic spectrum can find joy, fulfillment, and a feeling of purpose through these activities. Allowing these hobbies to blossom allows parents to enable their children to pursue their passions and skills.

Autism's particular interests frequently provide opportunities for self-expression and creativity. They enable people to delve deeply into a specific topic or activity, gaining considerable knowledge and competence. This focused exploration can result in a variety of advantages, including higher confidence, better social connections, and improved problem-solving abilities.

Furthermore, autistic-specific interests can provide motivation and involvement. They can help people with autism find meaning in their lives and feel accomplished. Recognizing and respecting these interests allows parents to foster a good environment that honors their child's distinct talents and abilities.

Encouraging and supporting special interests

Encouraging and supporting autism-specific hobbies is critical for a child's growth and well-being. By encouraging these hobbies, parents can help their children thrive and realize their full potential.

Here are various approaches for doing so:

- Active Engagement: Maintain an active interest in your child's specific interests. Demonstrate genuine curiosity and invite them to share their knowledge and experiences. By actively participating in their interests, you show your support and open up opportunities for genuine friendships.

- Providing Resources: Make available resources and materials that support your child's interests. This could include books, movies, and educational resources. By giving your child access to these materials, you may help them extend their knowledge and pursue their passion.

- Facilitating Social Opportunities: Seek out social opportunities based on your child's specific interests. This could include joining clubs, groups, or online forums to connect with others who share their interests. Socializing with people who share similar interests might help you feel more connected and form meaningful friendships.

- Setting goals: Encourage your youngster to develop goals based on their specific interests. Help them break down enormous ambitions into smaller, more manageable steps. This method might boost their sense of success and create a sense of purpose for their future development.

Recognizing and supporting autism-specific interests allows parents to establish an open and supportive atmosphere in which their child can thrive. These interests can reveal latent talents and create a distinct path for personal and social development. Parents may encourage and support their children's passion and help them thrive on the autism spectrum.

Benefits of Utilizing Autism Special Interests Harnessing and appreciating special interests can result in several benefits for those on the autism spectrum. These specialized interests can be an effective instrument for personal development and advancement.

Let's look at some of the primary benefits of fostering and supporting autistic-specific interests.

Developing Skills and Expertise Autism's unique interests typically feature strong intensity and passion for a certain subject or activity. This deep level of engagement permits persons on the autistic spectrum to build considerable knowledge and competence in their chosen areas of interest.

By promoting and nurturing these specific interests, individuals can strengthen their talents and become experts in their chosen fields. This can offer up prospects for personal and professional growth, as well as potential career pathways.

Ways Autism Special Interests Improve self-esteem and confidence
Feeling valued and respected.

Developing a sense of identity

Creating a support network.

Achieving goals and milestones

Overcoming challenges

Embracing uniqueness Individuals on the autism spectrum can benefit much from harnessing and embracing autism-specific interests. Parents, educators, and caregivers must foster an atmosphere that fosters and supports these interests, allowing individuals to develop and realize their full potential.

Nurturing Autism Special Interests

To accommodate people with autism and their specific interests, a supportive and inclusive atmosphere is required. The three important components of developing autistic special interests: fostering a supportive environment, balancing special interests with other activities, and encouraging discovery and growth.

Creating a supportive environment

Creating a supportive environment is vital for those with autism to feel comfortable and supported in following their specific interests.

Here are some techniques to foster such an environment: Acceptance and Understanding: Foster an atmosphere of acceptance and tolerance by educating yourself and others about autism and its distinctive characteristics. This helps build a pleasant and inclusive environment that embraces diversity.

Open Communication: Encourage open conversation to understand and respect an individual's specific interests. This requires actively listening, exhibiting real interest, and engaging in meaningful conversations to foster a sense of validation and connection.

Safe spaces: Create safe areas where people with autism can freely express and participate in their unique interests without fear of being judged or interrupted. These specialized places may include a quiet room, a separate office, or a specific area for their preferred pastimes.

Balancing Special Interests and Other Activities
While unique hobbies are vital for people with autism, it's also important to maintain a balance of other activities.

Here are some suggestions for reaching this balance:
Structured Routine: Create a planned regimen that includes time for hobbies as well as other important tasks like schoolwork, self-care, social connections, and physical exercise. This helps people create a well-rounded routine and encourages a good balance between their unique interests and other elements of life.

Flexibility: Allow for scheduling flexibility to meet unique interests while still ensuring that other obligations are met. This adaptability allows people with autism to keep their involvement and passion for their specific interests while also participating in other activities.

Supportive Guidance: Provide supportive assistance to individuals as they pursue new interests and activities outside of their major particular interest. Encourage them to try new things, join clubs or groups based on their specific interests, and participate in different experiences that extend their perspectives.

Encouraging exploration and growth

Encouraging discovery and growth in the area of unique interests is critical to the development and well-being of people with autism.

Here are some techniques to promote exploration and growth:

Exposure to new aspects: Encourage people to explore many aspects of their specific interests. This can include researching related topics, experimenting with new techniques or ideas, or working on collaborative projects with individuals who have similar interests.

Providing Resources: Ensure that students have access to resources such as books, online platforms, workshops, and community programs that allow them to learn, build skills, and network in their area of interest. This encourages constant growth and knowledge expansion.

Celebrating Achievements: Recognize and celebrate successes, milestones, and development in special interests.

Positive reinforcement and encouragement are extremely effective in increasing self-esteem and motivation. Individuals with autism can thrive and fully embrace their unique passions and talents by providing a supportive atmosphere that balances specific interests with other activities, as well as fostering exploration and progress.

Working with professionals and therapists
Collaboration with professionals and therapists can be quite beneficial in harnessing and promoting autism-specific interests. These professionals can provide significant information and assistance to people with autism as they explore and develop their specific interests.

Here are a few ways that professionals and therapists can help: Collaboration with Therapists Therapists who specialize in working with people on the autism spectrum can work with parents and individuals to optimize the benefits of autism-specific interests. Therapists can learn about an individual's strengths and motivations by sharing information about specific interests and their positive influence. This partnership allows therapists to personalize their therapies and tactics to the individual's specific interests, making therapy more interesting and effective.

Integrating Special Interests into Therapy Sessions
Integrating autism-specific hobbies into therapy sessions can improve the overall experience and results. Therapists can use the individual's specific interests in a variety of ways, such as rewards, incorporating them into therapeutic activities, and facilitating communication and social relationships.

Using the individual's love and excitement for their unique hobbies, therapists can create a more engaging and inspiring treatment setting.

Seeking professional guidance and advice
Parents and people can seek professional help and advice on how to support and nurture autism special interests. Professionals such as psychologists, behavior analyzers, and educational specialists can offer insights and solutions to help people pursue their specific interests in a healthy and balanced manner. They can also provide advice on identifying chances for growth and development, setting realistic goals, and dealing with any obstacles that may arise.

Working cooperatively with professionals and therapists, parents and individuals can ensure that autism-specific interests are cultivated in a positive and useful manner. These specialists' experience and assistance can help people with autism thrive and maximize their unique passions and abilities.

Autism special interests are a prevalent and significant feature of the illness. While they can be challenging, they also provide numerous benefits to people with autism. Understanding and supporting these interests allows people with autism to grow and attain their full potential.

CHAPTER 10

Physical Health Considerations For People With Autism

Physical health is an important part of overall well-being, and it can have a substantial impact on the quality of life for people with autism. While autism is primarily defined by impairments in social communication and behavior, people on the spectrum frequently suffer distinct physical health difficulties that must be carefully monitored and managed.

This section delves into the numerous physical health considerations for people with autism and presents techniques for effectively addressing these challenges.

Common Physical Health Concerns in Autism

1. Gastrointestinal (GI) Problems.
Prevalence: Many people with autism have gastrointestinal problems, including chronic

constipation, diarrhea, stomach pain, and gastroesophageal reflux disease (GERD).

Impact: GI issues can be quite uncomfortable and hurt behavior and mood.

Management Strategy: Dietary changes, such as increasing fiber consumption, can help relieve symptoms.

Probiotics and certain dietary therapies (such as gluten-free or casein-free diets) may benefit some people.

Healthcare professionals suggest regular medical evaluations and treatments.

2. Sleep Disorders:

Prevalence: Sleep disruptions are prevalent, including trouble falling asleep, frequent night awakenings, and inconsistent sleep patterns.

Impact: Poor sleep can exacerbate behavioral disorders, decrease cognitive performance, and lower general well-being.

Management Strategy: Creating a consistent nighttime routine and sleeping environment. Behavioral therapies for insomnia include cognitive-behavioral therapy (CBT-I).

Talk to your doctor about the possibility of using melatonin or other sleep aids.

3. Nutritional Deficiencies.

Prevalence: Picky eating habits and restrictive diets might result in nutritional deficits.- Impact: Vitamin and mineral deficiencies can impair growth, energy levels, and overall health.

Management Strategies:
Nutritional assessments performed by a trained dietitian.

Incorporating a wide range of nutrient-dense foods into the diet.

Supplementation as needed, under the supervision of a healthcare expert.

4. Seizure Disorders:
Prevalence: Epilepsy is more common among people with autism than in the general population.

Impact: Seizures can range from mild to severe and may necessitate continuing medical treatment.

Management strategies include regular neurological exams and monitoring.

Medication management and modifications as necessary.

Safety precautions to protect people during seizures.

5. Difficulties with motor coordination.
Prevalence: Many people with autism struggle with motor skills, especially fine and gross motor coordination.- Impact: Difficulties can interfere with daily tasks like handwriting, dressing, and engaging in sports.

Management Strategies:
Occupational therapy can enhance fine motor skills and coordination.

Physical therapy can help improve gross motor skills and general physical fitness.

Adaptive equipment and changes to promote independence.

General Health and Wellness Strategies

1. Regular medical checks.
Check-ups: Ensure regular health screenings and preventive care.

Monitor growth and development and respond quickly to any emergent health concerns.

2. Physical Activity: Encourage regular physical exercise based on the individual's interests and ability. Swimming, cycling, and team sports are all activities that can help you stay physically and socially active.

3. Healthy Diet: Encourage a healthy diet that includes a range of fruits, vegetables, whole grains, and lean proteins.

Address fussy eating habits with gradual exposure to new foods and positive reinforcement.

4. Hydration: Maintain proper fluid intake, especially for people who have limited verbal communication and may struggle to convey thirst.

5. Personal Hygiene: Teach and enforce excellent personal hygiene habits, such as frequent handwashing, dental care, and bathing.

6. Stress management: Practice stress-relieving activities like yoga, mindfulness, and sensory-friendly relaxation techniques.

Identify and address sources of stress that may be affecting physical health.

Collaboration with healthcare providers

1. Multidisciplinary Approach: Work with a group of healthcare providers that includes primary care physicians, neurologists, gastroenterologists, nutritionists, and therapists.

Create a thorough, individualized healthcare plan.

2. Communication: Maintain open and continuing conversation with your healthcare practitioner.

Share your observations and concerns about the individual's physical health, as well as any behavioral or symptom changes.

3. Education and Advocacy: Familiarize yourself with prevalent health conditions related to autism.

Advocate for proper medical care and support services.

Meeting the physical health needs of people with autism necessitates a proactive, knowledgeable, and collaborative approach.

Caregivers and healthcare providers can dramatically improve the overall well-being and quality of life for people on the autism spectrum by identifying common health concerns and applying appropriate management measures. Prioritizing physical health is an important step toward enabling people with autism to enjoy healthy, fulfilling lives.

CHAPTER 11

Maintaining Your Mental Wellness

Many autistic persons struggle with their mental health; this is a normal experience. There are numerous things you may do to boost your mental health and overall well-being.

Some of these include:

- Following a routine Even little changes might cause anxiety and stress. Try incorporating a schedule into your day to offer you more structure.

- Physical activity. Physical activity can be extremely good for one's mental health. Including a short stroll or any exercise, such as swimming, in your daily routine can help you achieve this.

- Eating and Drinking A well-balanced diet allows the body to function more efficiently and might make you feel more awake. Experiment with different foods and food groups, cooked or prepared in various ways, until you find something you enjoy. If you struggle to remember when to eat or drink, adding reminders to your schedule can help. If you're having trouble with your diet, talk to your doctor for support and advice.

- Wear headphones, earplugs, or ear defenders. Sensory overload can be challenging for autistic persons. Wearing headphones, earplugs, or ear defenders can effectively filter out sounds.

- Self-soothing box. Using a self-soothing box can help you calm and relax, especially during times of high stress.

- Keep a journal. Keeping a journal can be a terrific way to communicate your feelings.

- Try recording your ideas after each day. You can also include drawings and images if you desire.

- Practicing mindfulness helps alleviate stress, anxiety, and sadness. A daily mindfulness practice can increase emotions of peace and relaxation.

Get a decent night's sleep. A good night's sleep allows the body to unwind and process the day's activities. If you have trouble sleeping.

Every person is unique; using different tactics can help you figure out what works best for you. If you are struggling or concerned about your mental health, speak with your doctor to seek some assistance and advice. Autism is not a mental health issue, although autistic persons can experience excellent and negative mental health just like everyone else. There are things you can do to help, such as talking to others and seeking professional treatment if necessary.

CHAPTER 12

Importance Of Self-care For Autistic People: Strategies For Practicing Self-Care And Building Resilience

Throughout history, people have attempted to ensure their safety, health, and well-being. People have practiced rituals, consumed specialized meals or herbal treatments, and passed down knowledge of health-enhancing practices from generation to generation. However, self-care was not well defined until the late twentieth century.

The rise in chronic disease rates played a major role in society realizing the significance of actively and consciously caring for oneself, which led to a broader understanding of the notion of self-care. What is self-care? Self-care is referred to as "the ability to care for oneself through awareness, self-control, and self-reliance to achieve, sustain, or promote good health and well-being." Self-care refers to the ability to prioritize one's own needs. experiences, and habits while taking specific measures to promote their physical, emotional, and total well-being.

Self-care for autistic people Self-care is essential for everyone. It is especially crucial for individuals with autism spectrum conditions. Self-care improves the quality of life and overall well-being.

People with autism face far more pressures in their daily lives than neurotypical people. They frequently experience sensory overload, problems in social situations, difficulties managing daily obligations, co-occurring mental disorders such as anxiety or depression, and other stresses and stressors that many others do not have to deal with regularly.

Strengthening self-care skills can help people with autism cope with the challenges and stressors they face. Those who care for and support autistic persons, such as parents, caretakers, and therapists, can also assist them acquire self-care skills.

Strategies to Practice Self-Care

Let's look at some techniques for practicing self-care for people with autism.

- Connect with others. Although many people with autism struggle with relationships and social interactions, it can be advantageous for them to have at least one or two persons with whom they can connect regularly. Connecting with people promotes personal well-being by minimizing feelings of loneliness, instilling a sense of caring, and encouraging participation in further self-care practices to improve health and well-being.

- Find Relaxing Activities. People with autism benefit greatly from engaging in relaxing and calming activities. This helps to control one's emotions. It also helps control the nervous system. Relaxing activities can help people manage stress while also improving their mental health and well-being. The precise activity will vary depending on the person. It might be challenging for persons with autism to decide what hobbies they wish to pursue. They may be unsure of what hobbies they enjoy relaxing in, or they may struggle to begin an activity. It can be beneficial to try out several things to see what you enjoy the most.

Care For One's Body

Self-care entails taking care of one's physical well-being, which includes actions like showering, brushing one's teeth, combing one's hair, and any other behaviors related to personal hygiene and having a clean, healthy body.

People with autism frequently do better when there is a structure in place for the things they must complete regularly. They frequently perform well with routines. To assist self-care, people with autism should create a strategy that works for them. This could include showering on specified days of the week, brushing their teeth at the same time every day, and caring for their hair at set times in a consistent daily regimen.

Pursue Special Interests. Self-care includes sustaining your mental health. To accomplish this, a person may engage in activities that they are enthusiastic about. This is similar to the advice we made before about engaging in soothing activities. However, this varies because some people may have distinct interests that are not particularly soothing or tranquil.

Specific soothing activities that can help someone manage stress and stay calm may not be related to their interests. One of the defining characteristics of the autism spectrum condition is that the individual may have unique interests or subjects and activities with which they strongly connect and love spending time. These activities should become a regular part of their lifestyle.

Explore your mental health. People with autism should regularly check in with themselves regarding their mental health. This can be performed in several ways. People can, for example, devote some quiet time to self-reflection. They could also keep a notebook on what is going through their mind. People with autism frequently have co-occurring mental problems, such as anxiety or depression. If this is a concern, therapy may be a useful resource.

Developing Resilience for People with Autism
Stress and obstacles are unavoidable parts of life. The ability to recover and deal with hardship is known as resilience. Resilience is related to how we positively approach problems.

Building resilience can help people with autism improve their health and well-being. Building resilience can help people with autism navigate life's stressors and obstacles more successfully. This increased resilience boosts self-esteem, reduces anxiety, helps with social situations, and facilitates the acquisition of new abilities. Building resilience requires practice. Being effective in some activities is one method to develop resilience. People with autism can apply this method by taking incremental steps toward a larger aim.

By achieving these small victories, the individual can develop resilience while learning something new. When faced with a tough task, people with autism may become easily discouraged. However, it can be beneficial for them to remember (and for others who care for them to remind them) that it is okay to struggle with something. That doesn't always imply you shouldn't try something.

People can achieve success even with challenging projects if they have the correct assistance and strategy, as well as if they break them down into smaller, more manageable pieces. It is also acceptable to seek assistance and try again when faced with a difficult or unpleasant situation.

Building resilience for persons with autism is another strategy to promote self-care and is an important part of achieving a high quality of life.

CHAPTER 13

Developing Leisure Activities For Autistic People

Everyone's life revolves around leisure activities. Participating in engaging and fascinating activities improves a person's well-being, happiness, and life satisfaction. Leisure activities can be done alone or with others, at home or in the community.

We learn activities by seeing others, taking lessons, joining clubs, reading directions, or just trying. For those on the autism spectrum, establishing leisure activities and talents can be more difficult because skills are rarely learned by informal observation or imitation of others. Their interests evolve in their unique way.

Materials may be utilized in unclear ways, and they may be employed primarily for their sensory properties. Skills learned in one activity may not be applicable in another.

Why is it vital to develop leisure skills?
Challenging behaviors are frequently lessened when a person engages in personally rewarding leisure activities. The capacity to entertain oneself can help an individual relieve stress at home and in the community. There are also social benefits. Leisure skills and interests can bring together others who share the same passion. An activity brings together people who have a common interest and like discussing it.

My son, David, enjoys drumming and routinely attends drum circles. He meets others who adore drumming and they all make music together. Exposure to a diverse range of activities and experiences broadens interests. Interests will change over time, so it is critical to continue broadening experiences for growth and development.

Characteristics That Make Leisure Materials and Activities More Successful
While everyone has different preferences, the following characteristics might help make activities more meaningful and successful. Understanding an activity, the purpose of things, and what to do with them might be tough.

Here are some ideas for making things more understandable:

1. Static rules

2. Clearly defined beginning and end

3. Predictable or repeatable quality

4. Clear visual representation of tasks

5. Minimal verbal instructions

6. Structured Activities

Reactive

Reactive materials offer reinforcement via sensory feedback. This indicates that when you do an action, something happens that changes the appearance. Examples include lights, music, movement, and tactile sense.

Electronic and computer games provide this type of feedback, albeit it might be difficult to control the time spent on these gadgets.

Music can also increase interest.

Comfortable

To promote comfort, tasks should be challenging but not overly exciting, and appropriate for the individual's skill level. Low need for complicated social contact
Possibility for a sense of control or mastery

Active Young children require activities that require gross motor abilities, such as climbing, running, and jumping. Swinging and swimming are two good examples of rhythmic activities.

Physical activity is essential for people of all ages because it reduces stress, builds muscle, and increases flexibility and balance. Regular exercise can help you get a better night's sleep.

Visual-Spatial Repetitive manipulation of objects, arranging things in order, or fitting objects into spaces can be extremely motivating. Some numerous toys and activities give these characteristics, such as puzzles.

How Can We Find Out What A Person Enjoys Doing? It's also vital to consider what your family and friends enjoy doing, as they typically supply more options for activities. My son David enjoys audio tours, so we visit historical sites and museums with audio guides. David will spend hours staring at artwork if he can press a button and hear the story behind them. He does not show the same degree of curiosity without the audio guidance. Some families enjoy sports, concerts, nature walks, cooking, travel, historical places, and gyms - the possibilities are unlimited. Doing things that the family enjoys provides more opportunities for the person with ASD to practice, participate, and develop skills.

Conclusion

As we reach the end of this book, it's important to reflect on our journey together. This book was written to educate, support, and inspire everyone involved in the lives of people with autism. Autism is a lifelong journey with both unique challenges and exceptional accomplishments.

Understanding, supporting, and empowering people with autism is a process that evolves with each individual's growth and circumstances.

My goal is to continue creating environments in which persons with autism can thrive by highlighting their strengths and satisfying their needs. Continue your journey of understanding and empowerment.

The ideas and answers provided in this book aim to lay the framework for continued learning and development. As our understanding of autism evolves via continued research and lived experiences, we must stay open to new ideas and approaches.

The future holds promising developments in autism research, therapies, and societal attitudes that will supplement my efforts to help and empower persons with autism.

I encourage you to continue participating in the autistic community, whether through support groups, professional networks, or advocacy organizations. Collaboration and shared experiences are powerful tools for building a more inclusive and supportive community.

Final Thoughts And Encouragement

Every individual with autism is a unique and valuable member of our community. Their perspectives, abilities, and potential enrich the tapestry of human diversity. Understanding autism and providing thoughtful, targeted support can help these people realize their full potential.

Remember that the route beyond autism entails more than just overcoming barriers; it also entails acknowledging victories, developing strengths, and seeing a future in which every person with autism can flourish. Your dedication to learning, supporting, and empowering makes a tremendous difference on this journey.

Thank you for joining me on this adventure. Together, we can create a society in which people with autism are not only recognized and supported, but also fully empowered to lead fulfilling and happy lives. The journey continues, and with your dedication, the opportunities are limitless.

www.ingramcontent.com/pod-product-compliance
Lightning Source LLC
Chambersburg PA
CBHW061654250726
48659CB00004B/1489